PEOPLES AND THEIR ENVIRONMENTS ™

PEOPLES OF THE SAVANNA

Robert Low

The Rosen Publishing Group's
PowerKids Press™
New York

Published in 1996, 2003 by The Rosen Publishing Group, Inc.
29 East 21st Street, New York, NY 10010

Copyright © 1996, 2003 by The Rosen Publishing Group, Inc.

All rights reserved. No part of this book may be reproduced in any form without permission in writing from the publisher, except by a reviewer.

Revised Edition 2003

Editor: Natashya Wilson
Book Design: Kim Sonsky
Text Revisions: Magdalena Alagna

Photo Credits: Cover, p. 15 © Phyllis Galembo; p. 4 © Charles O'Rear/CORBIS; p. 12 © Dean Jacobson; p. 7 © David Cimino/International Stock; p. 8 © Joe McDonald/CORBIS; p. 11 © G. E. Pakenham/International Stock; pp. 16, 20 © Yann Arthus-Bertrand/CORBIS; p. 19 © Hilde Hendrikson.

Low, Robert, 1952–
    Peoples of the Savanna / Robert Low.
       p.   cm. — (Peoples and their environments)
    Includes index.
    Summary: Describes the interrelationship between the peoples and the plants and animals of the African grasslands.
    ISBN 0-8239-6811-1
    1. Human geography—Africa—Juvenile literature. 2. Savannas—Africa—Juvenile literature. 3. Ethnology—Africa—Juvenile literature. 4. Human geography—Juvenile literature. [1. Savanna ecology. 2. Ecology.] I. Title. II. Series: Low Robert, 1952– Peoples and their environments.
GF701.L69 1996
304.2'3'09609153—dc20
                                            96-14279
                                              CIP
                                             AC

Manufactured in the United States of America

Contents

What Is a Savanna?

A savanna is a large area of grassland. It stretches as far as the eye can see. The land can be flat or hilly. Trees and bushes grow here and there. Savannas are warm almost all year. The rainy season is during the summer. Long ago, many people lived on savannas in different places, such as South America, Australia, Southeast Asia, and Africa. As people developed **agriculture**, many left the savannas to work on farms in small communities. After the rise of industry, some people chose to live in cities.

◄ This flat African savanna has a few trees growing on it.

The Peoples of the Savanna

Some peoples still live on savannas. Many of these peoples are in Africa. The **Fulani** live a simple life on the savanna in West Africa. Many own a few cows or goats to provide milk and cheese for their families.

The **Maasai** live and raise cattle on the savanna in East Africa. They build their houses using mud, sticks, grass, and cow dung. They eat the meat and drink the milk of their cattle.

The **Herero** live on the savanna in southern Africa. They raise cattle, too.

The Maasai still live on the savanna in East Africa. ▶
Inset: This map shows where the Maasai live in Africa.

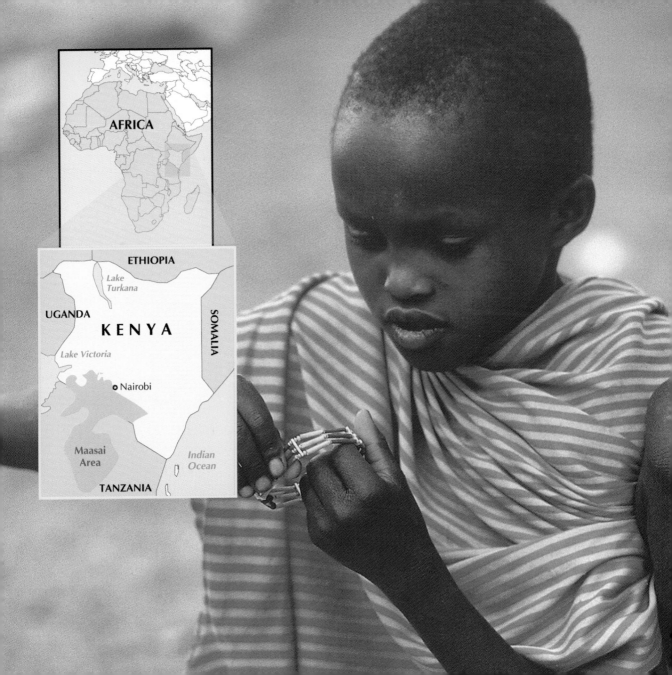

AFRICA

ETHIOPIA

Lake
Turkana

UGANDA

KENYA

SOMALIA

Lake Victoria

Nairobi

Maasai
Area

Indian
Ocean

TANZANIA

Plants and Animals

On the savanna, some grasses grow as high as 15 feet (5 m)! Others are only 1 foot (30 cm) tall. Most bushes and trees have small leaves and thorns. The Maasai use these thorny trees and bushes to build fences.

Zebras, giraffes, and other animals of the African savannas eat grass. The cattle that the Herero, Maasai, and Fulani raise also eat grass. Animals of the savanna are hunted by **predators**, such as lions and leopards, which also live on the savanna.

◀ Zebras are one of the many types of animals that feed on the grasses of the savanna.

Raising Cattle

Savannas are good places to raise cattle because there is so much grass. People raise cattle for their meat and their milk. Some peoples, such as the Maasai, trade the milk for things such as beads or grain. Long ago all Fulani and Maasai were **nomads**. They moved from place to place with their herds. When the cattle had eaten all the grass in one area, the Fulani or the Maasai would move to a new area. Today some Fulani and Maasai stay in one place year-round, raising cattle and growing crops, as do the Herero.

Some Maasai still move across the savanna with their cattle. ▶

Food on the Savanna

The Maasai's main food is milk. They buy potatoes, bread, and sugar from stores located in villages to which they can walk from the savanna. The Maasai eat the meat of their cattle only during special ceremonies.

Many Fulani live mostly on milk, cheese, yogurt, and other dairy products. They eat beef on special occasions. They trade their dairy products for grain, fruit, and other foods.

The Herero eat the meat of their cattle and drink the milk. They also grow grain and vegetables or buy them at markets.

◀ The Herero store the milk from their cows in large, hollow gourds.

Clothing

Clothing worn on the savanna is often brightly colored. Fulani women wear wraps or dresses with fancy designs. They are known for their beautiful jewelry and hairstyles. Fulani men usually wear a shirt and pants or a robe. Maasai men and women often wear red or brown wraps and beaded jewelry. Long ago, the Herero wore leather clothing. When Europeans arrived around 1850, many Herero began to wear European-style clothes. Today, Herero women wear long dresses and matching head coverings.

Fulani women often wear bright, beautiful dresses, jewelry, and head coverings. ▶

Homes

Homes on the savanna are often built with natural materials. When traveling with their herds, Fulani men and women make shelters from straw mats or branches and leaves. Maasai women are the ones who build and care for their homes. They build round homes with wood, grass, mud, and cow dung. The Maasai use thorny bushes to build fences around their villages. Herero women also build the houses. Long ago, their homes were made of sand and cow dung. Today many Herero houses are built with wood and metal.

◀ This Maasai woman is building a hut from mud and straw while her children watch. The mud and straw are dried on the hut's wooden frame.

Families and Communities

Each savanna people has its own way of life. Maasai who travel with their cattle live in groups of about six families. Each nomadic Fulani family travels alone with its herd. Other Fulani live in villages. The Fulani have ceremonies for events such as marriages, births, and deaths. Many Herero live in **homesteads**. A homestead includes the homes of all the relatives in a family. Several homesteads make up a village. The cattle are kept in **outposts** around the village.

The Herero live in homesteads with all their relatives. ▶

CHILDREN OF THE SAVANNA

Children on the savanna learn about the role that they are expected to have in their community by watching their parents and family members. They also help with the daily chores. Fulani boys help to herd cattle from one place to the next. Maasai boys prepare to become great warriors, able to protect their families from harm. Maasai, Fulani, and Herero girls all help their mothers build homes, milk cows, cook, and take care of younger children.

◀ This Maasai child is mixing cattle blood. The blood is mixed with either milk or fat. The Maasai drink the blood in special cases. For instance, the sick will drink blood to gain strength.

Changing Lives

Today it is hard for the peoples of the savanna to keep their traditional ways of life. Changes in Earth's climate have made the savanna less **fertile**. Crops are becoming harder to grow. It is harder than ever to raise cattle on the savanna's grasses. The Fulani and the Maasai no longer move around as much as they once did. The Herero have started new traditions, such as wearing a different type of clothing. All the peoples are learning new ways to live with the changes on the savanna.

Glossary

agriculture (A-grih-kul-cher) The science of growing crops and raising animals.

fertile (FER-tul) Good for growing things.

Fulani (foo-LAH-nee) A people who live in western Africa.

Herero (huh-REH-roh) A people who live in southern Africa.

homesteads (HOHM-stedz) Groups of homes.

Maasai (MAH-sy) A people who live in eastern Africa.

nomads (NOH-madz) People who move from place to place.

outposts (OWT-pohsts) A small settlement set up outside the main village.

predators (PREH-duh-terz) Animals that kill other animals for food.

Index

Web Sites

Due to the changing nature of Internet links, PowerKids Press has developed an online list of Web sites related to the subject of this book. This site is updated regularly. Please use this link to access the list:
www.powerkidslinks.com/pate/savan/